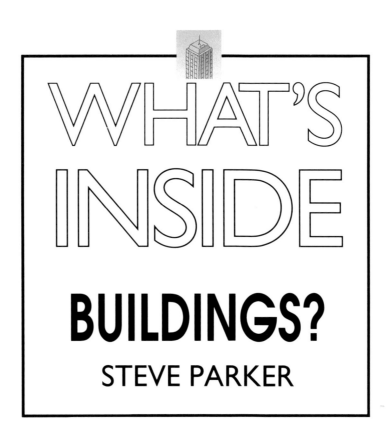

WHAT'S INSIDE

BUILDINGS?

STEVE PARKER

SIMON & SCHUSTER
YOUNG BOOKS

First published in 1993 by
Simon & Schuster Young Books

© 1993 Simon & Schuster Young Books

Simon & Schuster Young Books
Campus 400
Maylands Avenue
Hemel Hempstead
Hertfordshire
HP2 7EZ

A CIP catalogue record for this book is
available from the British Library

ISBN 0 7500 1315 X

Commissioning Editor: Thomas Keegan
Designer: John Kelly
Editor: Nicky Barber
Illustrators: Brian Watson, David Cook
(Linden Artists); Maltings Partnership;
Kevin Maddison
Typesetter:
Goodfellow & Egan, Cambridge
Printed and bound in Hong Kong

Contents

Introduction

Humans have constructed buildings since the earliest times. Prehistoric people moved from caves to shelters made out of branches and leaves. From about 10,000 years ago, people began to put up the first large, permanent buildings. These buildings marked the beginning of a settled way of life, and the start of villages, towns and cities. Today, the Earth's landscape is dotted with buildings of every shape and size.

TUNNELS
The Channel Tunnel will carry rail passengers between Britain and France. Other tunnels carry water, or sewage, or gas pipes.

A BRIDGE FOR WATER
Sometimes fresh water has to be carried over a gap to a town. This is done by an aqueduct, such as the Pont du Gard, built by the Romans near Nîmes, France in AD 19.

NOT JUST OFFICES
The John Hancock Center is unusual among very tall buildings, because it houses offices, shops, apartments, restaurants and and leisure facilities. It is called a 'multi-use' skyscraper. Its immense structure of steel girders is strengthened by diagonal pieces, called trusses.

THE SKYSCRAPER
The USA is the home of the skyscraper – the top ten highest ones are all there. The John Hancock Center in Chicago is 344 metres high, and has 100 storeys. It is the world's fifth tallest skyscraper.

John Hancock Center, Chicago

A dam holds back water in a reservoir, storing it for times of drought, and generating electricity from turbines spun by the energy of the moving water.

IS IT A BUILDING?
When is a building simply a structure? Usually, if people do not occupy it regularly or work or live there, then it is not a true building. The CN Tower in Toronto, Canada, is 553 metres high. But it is a very tall and elegant mast rather than a proper skyscraper.

CN Tower, Toronto

STADIA
Sports Stadia hold huge numbers of people.

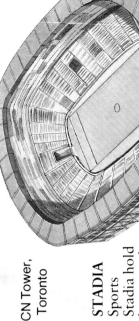

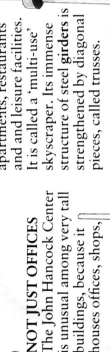

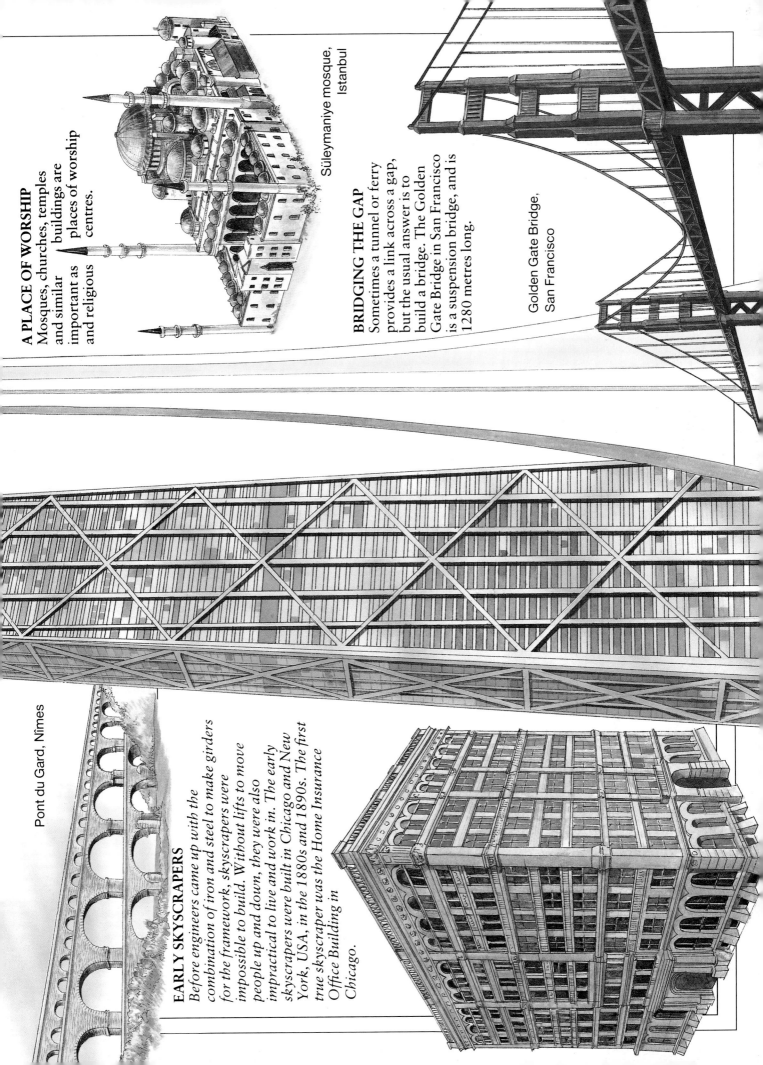

A PLACE OF WORSHIP
Mosques, churches, temples and similar buildings are important as places of worship and religious centres.

Süleymaniye mosque, Istanbul

BRIDGING THE GAP
Sometimes a tunnel or ferry provides a link across a gap, but the usual answer is to build a bridge. The Golden Gate Bridge in San Francisco is a suspension bridge, and is 1280 metres long.

Golden Gate Bridge, San Francisco

Pont du Gard, Nîmes

EARLY SKYSCRAPERS
Before engineers came up with the combination of iron and steel to make girders for the framework, skyscrapers were impossible to build. Without lifts to move people up and down, they were also impractical to live and work in. The early skyscrapers were built in Chicago and New York, USA, in the 1880s and 1890s. The first true skyscraper was the Home Insurance Office Building in Chicago.

First structures

In past times, huge structures were rarely built as places to live or work. Many of these structures had no practical use at all. They were symbols of various kinds – of success and power, wealth, and religion. The main building materials were stone blocks, cut and shaped and moved into position by teams of slave workers. A selection of the world's most amazing ancient buildings and structures is shown here.

EARLY PYRAMIDS

The pharaohs of Ancient Egypt built pyramids as tombs, to make sure that they would have a comfortable life after death. The Step Pyramid of King Zoser at Saqqara was the first to be built, constructed in 2650 BC. Originally it was surrounded by small buildings where people could worship the souls of the dead.

Ancient Egyptian measurements

Cubit

Palm

5 Palms = 1 Cubit

4 Fingers = 1 Palm

PLANS AND MEASUREMENTS

A giant structure such as a pyramid or statue cannot be made without preparation. The designers of these structures needed to know how to cut stone blocks, how many blocks were required, and exactly where to place them. As these early engineers learned how to plan the construction of buildings they developed systems of measuring and geometry.

The Colossus of Rhodes

Step Pyramid

Great Pyramid of Khufu

THE GREAT PYRAMID OF KHUFU

Erected in about 2500 BC at Giza, Egypt, the Great Pyramid of Khufu is the world's largest pyramid. Each side is 230 metres long, and the height would once have been 147 metres.

THE COLOSSUS OF RHODES

The Colossus of Rhodes was a giant bronze statue of the god Helios (of the Sun). It was completed around 280 BC. At 36 metres high, it was 20 times taller than an adult man, and it stood at the entrance to the city's harbour.

10

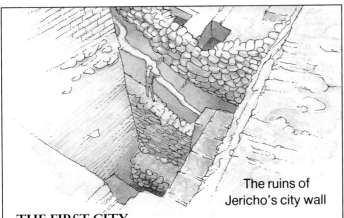

THE FIRST CITY
Jericho is the earliest city yet discovered. Its ruins date from over 10,000 years ago and are near the Dead Sea in the Middle East. The city wall was more than five metres high, and the site was occupied until about 3500 years ago.

The ruins of Jericho's city wall

THE TOWER OF BABEL
The Bible says that the Tower of Babel was built by Noah's descendants to bring all the peoples together in one place. But God turned their talk into nonsensical 'babble'.

The Tower of Babel

THE HANGING GARDENS OF BABYLON
The Hanging Gardens were supposedly built in Babylon around 570 BC by King Nebuchadnezzar II. Archaeologists have discovered ruins that may be the lower levels of the terraced gardens.

THE FIRST BUILDINGS
Fossilized remains from near Nice, France, show that our prehistoric ancestors *Homo erectus* may have constructed low huts out of branches, with stone bases. This was 400,000 years ago when the site, Terra Amata, was a Mediterranean beach.

The Hanging Gardens of Babylon

Stonehenge, England

STANDING STONES
Curious lines and circles of enormous standing stones were usually put up as part of the religious worship of the Sun and Moon. There have been stones at Stonehenge, near Salisbury, England, for almost 5000 years. They were erected by digging pits and toppling the stones into them.

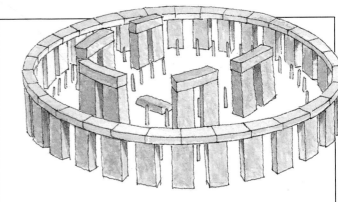

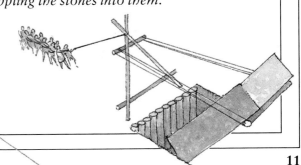

The basics of building

From the time of Ancient Greece and Rome, certain methods of construction and certain designs turn up again and again in building. The **column**, the **arch**, the **vault** and the **dome** are found in many large structures, which are almost always built of stone. These shapes provided strength and stability, and they could be designed into beautiful outlines and patterns.

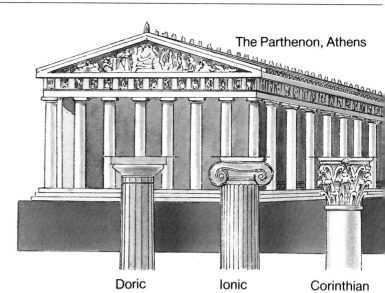

The Parthenon, Athens

Doric   Ionic   Corinthian

Pont du Gard, Nîmes

COLUMNS
A pillar can be square, rectangular or oval – but a column is always round. It supports the upper sections and roof of a building. Many Ancient Greek buildings were based on columns. A famous example is the Parthenon in Athens.

ARCHES
The Romans used the arch to construct big structures and buildings. The arch is excellent at supporting weight. This is because downward forces on it try to compress, or squash, its parts together, making it even stronger.

Wooden struts held the stones in place during construction.

THE ISLAMIC ARCH
The teardrop shape of the pointed arch or dome, often with a narrow base, is associated with mosques and other buildings of the Islamic world. The mosque is a place of worship for those following the Muslim religion.

Taj Mahal, Agra

VAULTS
The vault is like a series of arches joined together. It was the basic design used to support large roofs until new materials became available in the last two centuries. Many medieval churches have vaulted ceilings. The tunnel or **barrel vault** *is the simplest form. A groin, or cross vault, is formed where two tunnel vaults of the same size meet at right angles.*

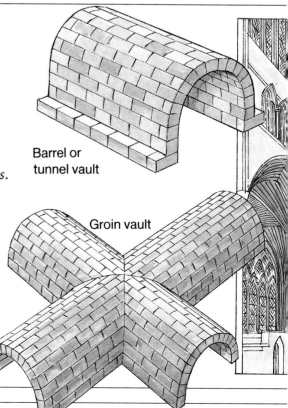

Barrel or tunnel vault

Groin vault

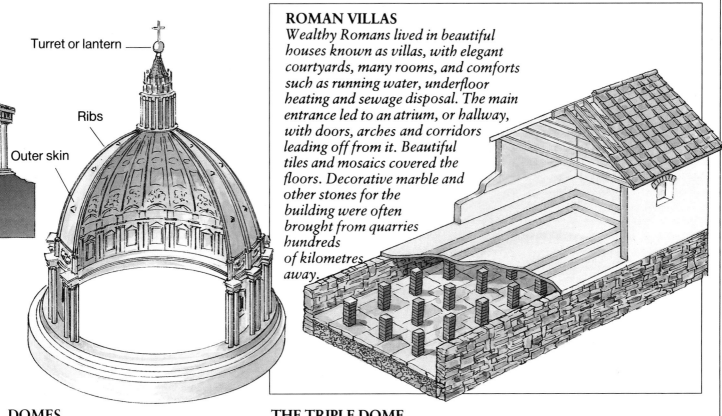

Turret or lantern

Ribs

Outer skin

ROMAN VILLAS

Wealthy Romans lived in beautiful houses known as villas, with elegant courtyards, many rooms, and comforts such as running water, underfloor heating and sewage disposal. The main entrance led to an atrium, or hallway, with doors, arches and corridors leading off from it. Beautiful tiles and mosaics covered the floors. Decorative marble and other stones for the building were often brought from quarries hundreds of kilometres away.

DOMES

The dome has the same advantages of strength with lightness as the arch. A dome is the main design used for covering large spaces without supporting columns below. The dome of St Peter's Basilica in the Vatican, Rome, Italy was completed in 1590.

THE TRIPLE DOME

St Paul's Cathedral in London, England, was begun in 1675 and finished in 1711. It has a dome 111 metres high. The architect of St Paul's, Sir Christopher Wren, based his design on the dome of St Peter's Basilica, but he included a middle dome with a cone shape. This meant the shallow inner dome formed a circular balcony at its apex, or top. Stairways lead between the outer and middle domes, among the wooden beams of the framework, to the turret at the top of the dome.

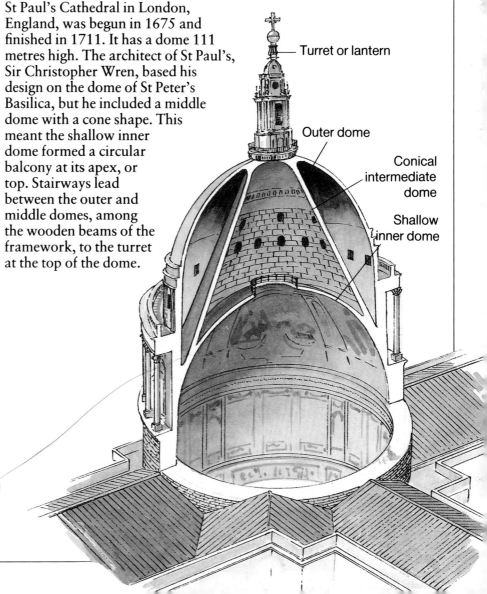

Turret or lantern

Outer dome

Conical intermediate dome

Shallow inner dome

Vaulted ceiling

Foundations and footings

You would not put a heavy stone building in the middle of a soft, boggy swamp. It might sink out of sight! This is an obvious example of the fact that any large structure needs a solid base, or firm foundation. The **foundations** of a building prevent it from sinking straight down. They also stop it falling over, since a strong wind blowing against a large structure produces huge sideways forces.

BASIC DESIGN
The earth under our feet may feel hard to us, but it becomes soft and squashy when pressed on by the hundreds of tonnes of weight of a building. There are several designs for foundations. Some are pillar-like piles sunk deep into the ground, others are walls that carry on below the surface, or even wide, flat rafts on which the whole building sits.

1 POURING THE PILES
Most piles are made from **concrete** with metal rods or a girder, inside. The site is excavated and holes drilled, and the concrete poured in.

2 UNDERGROUND SPACE
The piles, or the pillars on top of them, can sometimes be seen in the basement areas of a tall building. These basement areas are often useful for storage and parking.

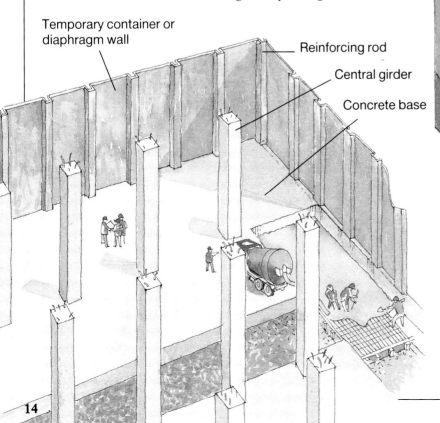

Temporary container or diaphragm wall

Reinforcing rod

Central girder

Concrete base

A FIRM BED
In New York solid rock lies just below the surface. This is called bedrock. Any heavy building can rest on the bedrock, on straight piles. Sometimes the rock is too near the surface. Holes may have to be blasted into it and the foundations set in so that they can cope with tilting and twisting forces on the building above.

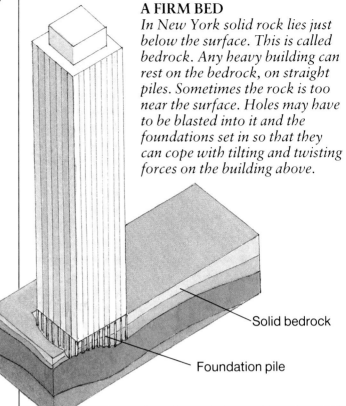

Solid bedrock

Foundation pile

Pile

PILES
Piles are underground supporting pillars. The NatWest Tower in London, England, has 375 of them. This skyscraper is 183 metres high, its main foundations are 18 metres deep, and there are 375 piles that go more than 40 metres below the surface. The piles prevent the tower from sinking down and tipping sideways in the soft London clay.

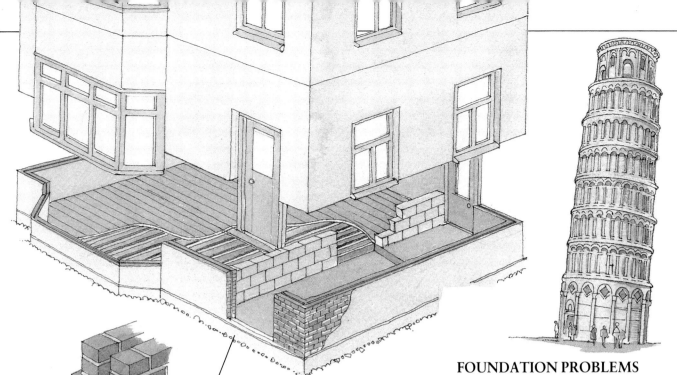

Concrete base

FOOTINGS
A typical ordinary house has **footings**, where the walls extend below the ground. The footings must be deep and wide enough to take the weight of the house above, depending on the type of soil and rock in the area. When the footings are complete, the shape of the house can be seen on the ground.

POURING FOOTINGS
After the site is marked out with pegs and string, trenches are dug for the footings. Hardcore (mixed bricks, stones and other rubble) is packed down in the bottom, then concrete is poured on the top. Metal rods, or bricks, may be left sticking out to fit into the walls. At the same time drains, pipes and **ducts** are installed so that the floors and footings will not have to be dug out later.

FOUNDATION PROBLEMS
The Leaning Tower of Pisa, in Italy, is a well-known example of what happens when foundations are not firm enough. It is an eight-storey bell tower, and it is 54 metres high. Even as it was being built, from 1175 to about 1350, it began to lean. It continues to do so, by around one millimetre more each year. It is now 5 metres from the true vertical. In 1993, a 600-tonne counterweight was fixed to one side, to stop the tower leaning over any more. Pisans did not want to make the tower upright again, otherwise their city would lose a valuable tourist attraction.

CONCRETE
Concrete is a combination of cement (limestone or chalk ground up with clay or shale), aggregate (stones) and water. It is the staple material used for foundations and footings. Concrete does not set and harden by drying out. The process of hardening is a chemical reaction, which is why concrete goes hard even under water.

DIGGING FOR PILES
There are several ways to make the hole for a pile. The piledriver (1) repeatedly lifts and drops a heavy weight on to a huge metal spike, driving it like a giant needle through the earth. A metal girder pile can be hammered directly into place, forcing the earth sideways (2). Or a corkscrew-like drill (3) cuts into the earth and removes it at the same time, leaving a clean hole.

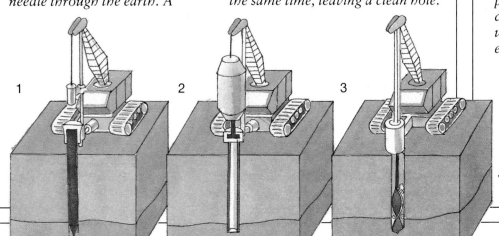

1   2   3

Cellars and basements

If the earth is taken away from between the foundations of a large building, a useful underground space is formed. Cellars, **crypts**, basements and similar areas have no natural light, so few people live or work there permanently. They are most useful for storage, security, and hiding the building's **services** such as water pipes, and heating ducts.

UNDER A CATHEDRAL

In a typical large church or cathedral, the space under the floor is a network of passages, rooms and chambers. Dark, secretive and secure, this underground warren has many uses. In times of war, people could be given sanctuary hiding behind false panels or in special secret rooms.

THE CRYPT

A crypt is an underground chamber in a church. It is usually at the eastern end of the building. It may house an entire chapel for special worship, or a simple altar for prayers.

CONSTANT CONDITIONS

Under the ground, away from the rain and seasons, the atmosphere in a cellar tends to stay much the same all year round. These conditions are ideal for storing wines and produce while they mature. Many of the French chateaus have enormous wine cellars.

IN MEMORY

Crypts may also contain tombs, and monuments to saints and officials connected to the church. The roof of a crypt is usually a barrel vault design (see page 18), which is why these types of underground chambers are sometimes known as vaults.

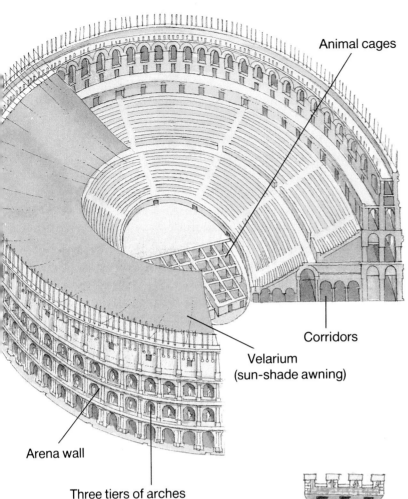

Animal cages

Corridors

Velarium
(sun-shade awning)

Arena wall

Three tiers of arches

THE COLOSSEUM

The Flavian Amphitheatre in Rome, Italy, is usually known as the Colosseum. It was completed in AD 80 by Titus, son of Vespasian, who began it in AD 69. The whole structure was 615 metres long, 156 metres wide and 45 metres high, and 50,000 spectators could sit around the arena. The arena was 86 metres long and 54 metres wide (about the size of an average soccer pitch), and part of its floor was made of thick wooden planks. For one entertainment the planks were taken away and the arena was flooded for a mock sea battle with real ships.

UNDER THE ARENA

The lower levels of the Colosseum housed prisons and cages. Animals such as lions and bulls were moved along sealed corridors, and brought up to the arena by lifting platforms with counter-balanced weights.

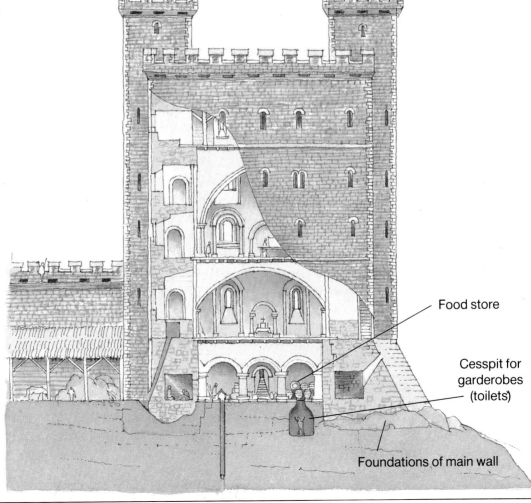

DUNGEONS AND PRISONS

In medieval times, the castle was a multi-purpose building. It was a home for living and eating, a prison, a fortress, and a storehouse for food and other supplies. The cool conditions in the cellar were best for keeping perishable foods. The dark, damp dungeons had thick stone walls with solid earth behind.

Food store

Cesspit for garderobes (toilets)

Foundations of main wall

The skeleton

In older buildings, the parts holding up the whole structure were the walls. In most modern skyscrapers, this has changed. The load-bearing part is the structural framework or 'skeleton' made of steel girders or, less commonly, concrete beams and pillars. The skeleton takes all the weight. The world's tallest skyscraper, the Sears Building in Chicago, has 80,000 tonnes of structural steel in its frame.

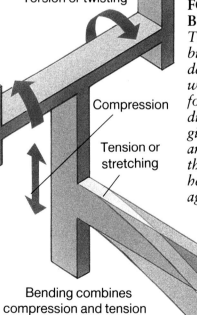

Tube or O-beam

I-beam

L-beam

GIRDERS
Steel is a strong metal yet it is light. To make the parts for a load-bearing frame it is formed into girders. Seen end-on, girders are usually made in shapes such as an L, an I or an O (a tube). These shapes combine strength with as little weight as possible.

Torsion or twisting

Compression

Tension or stretching

FORCES ON A BUILDING
The framework of a building must be designed to cope with enormous forces in several directions. Each girder is designed and positioned so that its longest side helps to push against the force.

Bending combines compression and tension

A tall skyscraper must resist sideways forces. Winds try to bend it with the force of thousands of tonnes. Strong winds make tall skyscrapers rock to and fro.

THE MODERN HIGH-RISE
When a tall building is being erected, the inner framework of steel beams and columns is constructed first. The outer walls, or **cladding**, are fixed on to the framework. The outer walls are usually made up of panels of regular sizes. The windows may be attached directly to the frame, or fitted into the panels later.

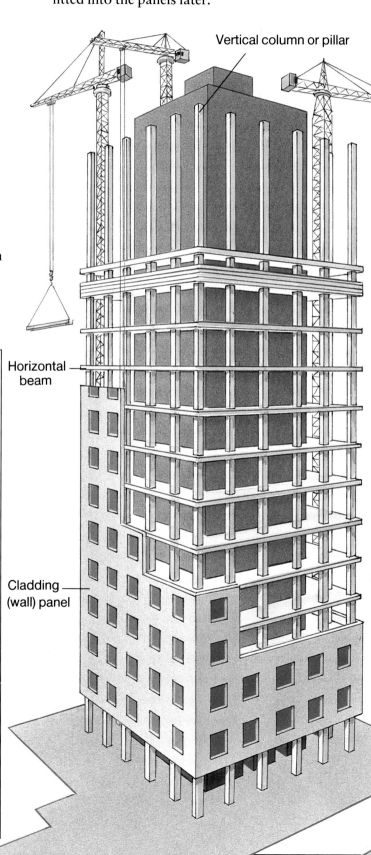

Vertical column or pillar

Horizontal beam

Cladding (wall) panel

Rivet inserted

Weld

Rivet flattened

Finished joint

JOINING STEEL
Steel and similar metals can be joined in various ways, according to the strength required. In welding, the two metals are heated so much that they melt and flow together, then cool and harden. A rivet is a small metal rod that is pushed through holes in each part, then flattened at the ends to hold the parts together.

THICK WALLS
The base of a large stone wall supports many tonnes of rock above, so it has to be wide and firm. In past times, the walls built around a castle or fort were many metres thick, and had very deep foundations.

Sentry pathway

Parapet

Body of wall

Sheer face with few handholds for climbing.

Ridge

Rafter

Eaves

TIMBER FRAMES
In times before iron and steel girders could be made, builders used timber to make the frames for houses, halls and barns. This is the frame of an English Tudor house from the 16th century. Oak was a favourite wood for building frames because it was heavy and strong. It also did not rot or decay too quickly. Two of the many types of joints, the mortise-and-tenon joint, and the halving or half-lap joint, are shown below.

member

T-halving joint

Mortise

Tenon

Mortise and tenon joint

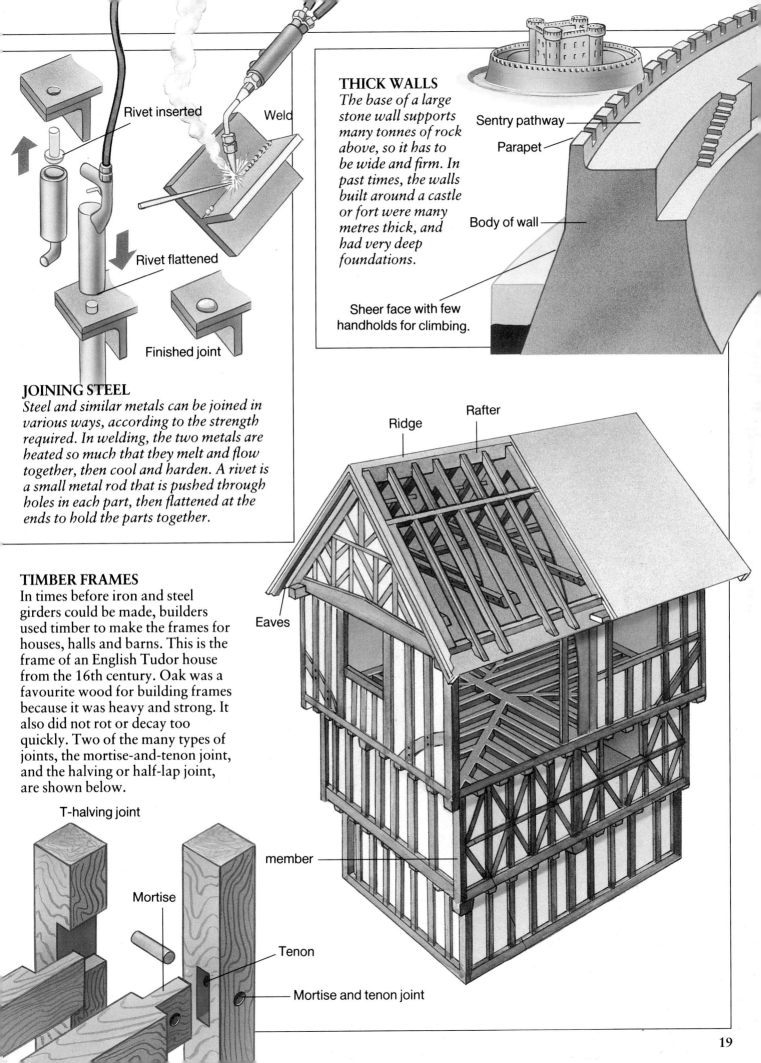

The business of buildings

The shape, design and construction of a building reflect its main purpose – and also the wealth of its owners. Any large structure, from a castle to a cathedral, from a theatre to a railway station, needs huge amounts of money, time, workers, skills and materials. In past times, kings and lords relied on the threat of their armies to provide all these. Today, a big building requires big business.

THE CASTLE
The stone castle was a fortress home for the medieval king, lord or duke. It was designed by architects and engineers, and built largely by local peasants. The castle was a symbol of the owner's wealth and influence, as well as being a home, and a safe retreat in case of attack by enemies.

ROOMS AT THE TOP
The routine of the castle centred around the needs of the lord and lady, who had the safest, least draughty and most spacious rooms. These were usually high in the building, so that the masters were 'above' their servants and soldiers.

Buttress walls

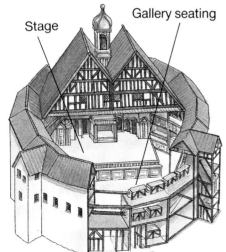

Stage

Gallery seating

THE THEATRE
The Globe Theatre in London was England's foremost playhouse from 1599 until it was demolished in 1644. It was owned and run by a combination of the rich and influential Burbage family, and a group of writers and actors known as Chamberlain's Men, which included William Shakespeare.

THE TOWN HOUSE
People often showed how rich and successful they were by owning several houses. Grand mansions in the countryside were for restful breaks, country parties, hunting and shooting. The town house was a base from which to do business, and to take in the pleasures of the city such as theatres and restaurants.

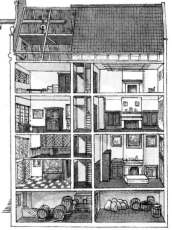

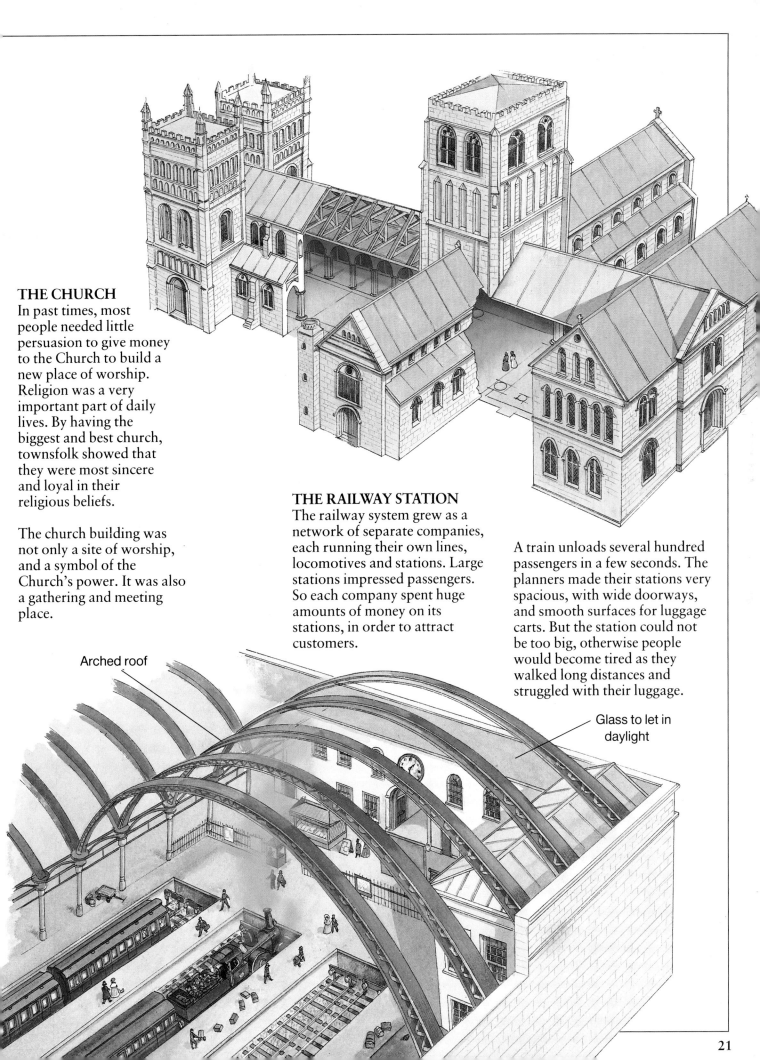

THE CHURCH

In past times, most people needed little persuasion to give money to the Church to build a new place of worship. Religion was a very important part of daily lives. By having the biggest and best church, townsfolk showed that they were most sincere and loyal in their religious beliefs.

The church building was not only a site of worship, and a symbol of the Church's power. It was also a gathering and meeting place.

THE RAILWAY STATION

The railway system grew as a network of separate companies, each running their own lines, locomotives and stations. Large stations impressed passengers. So each company spent huge amounts of money on its stations, in order to attract customers.

A train unloads several hundred passengers in a few seconds. The planners made their stations very spacious, with wide doorways, and smooth surfaces for luggage carts. But the station could not be too big, otherwise people would become tired as they walked long distances and struggled with their luggage.

Arched roof

Glass to let in daylight

Floors

A floor is something you walk on – and much more. In a modern multi-storey building it contains pipes and ducts for the services such as water, electricity, ventilation and **air-conditioning** (*see page 36*). It also forms the ceiling of the storey below. The floor structure must be light so as not to put too much load on the frame, yet it must be strong enough to take the weight of heavy furniture or machinery.

PARTS OF A FLOOR
This exploded view shows the various layers that make a typical floor in a modern skyscraper. The pattern is repeated for each storey, so that the parts can be made on a production line to save cost.

UNDER THE FLOOR COVERING
Under the carpet and foam underlay, there may be a layer of boards or panels, made from wood or a man-made material. These form a smooth, flat surface, but they can be taken up for maintenance and repairs.

DECKING
The main structural parts of a floor are sheets of metal called floor decking. These have ridges, sometimes in a grid pattern, to make them stiff yet light. They may have a layer of concrete poured on to them.

SERVICES
Electricity-supply wires, telecommunication wires, air ducts, and pipes for water and drainage are some of the services that run through the floor. They need to be out of the way – if they were laid on the floor itself, people would trip over them!

CEILING
Tiles cover the ceiling of the storey below. These absorb noise and they can be moved to change the layout of the lighting.

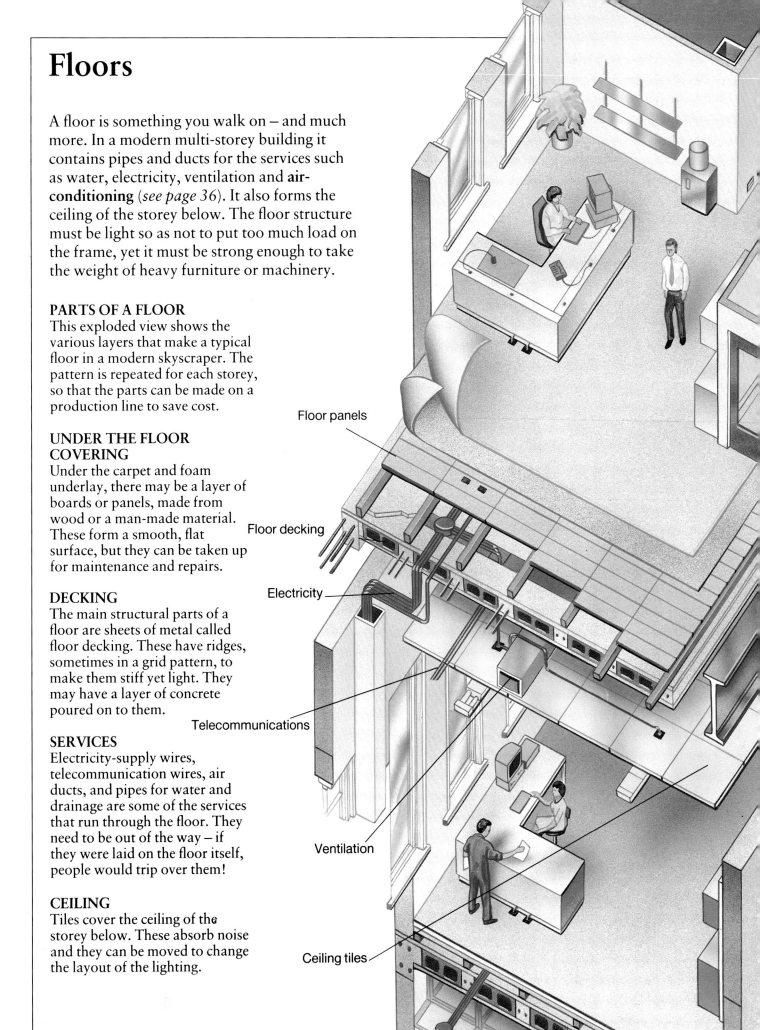

Floor panels

Floor decking

Electricity

Telecommunications

Ventilation

Ceiling tiles

A DOMESTIC FLOOR
*Many ordinary houses have a floor made of floorboards. These bend slightly when you walk on them, to make the floor more comfortable. They are supported by timber beams called **joists**, which run the opposite way to the boards. The joists are held away from the damp ground by brick supports.*

Joist

Floorboard

Brick support

GALLERIES
Some floors do not extend right across the building, but stick out only part of the way. These long thin floors are called galleries, and larger ones are **mezzanines**. They may be supported on beams that are fixed only at one end, known as cantilever beams. Or they can be supported by columns or pillars resting on the main floor below.

Cantilever beam

TYPES OF COVERING
There is a huge choice of floor coverings, each with its advantages and drawbacks. For example, stone tiles are very hard-wearing and easy to clean. But they are cold, and not comfortable for long periods of walking and standing

DECORATIVE FLOORS
The Romans were masters at making beautiful floors from patterns and mosaics of coloured stone tiles. Luckily, many of these survive to modern times. Some had underfloor heating, to make the tiles warm and heat the room above.

Carpet

Carpet tiles

Stone tiles

Synthetic tiles

Rubberized covering

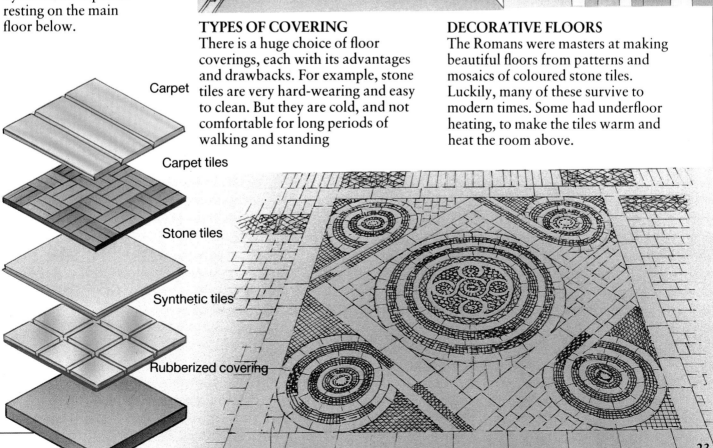

23

Walls

In older, larger buildings, such as cathedrals, the walls held up the load – the combined weights of the floors, furniture and people inside, and the roof on top. These walls are known as **load-bearing walls**, and they are immensely thick. Light was allowed in through large windows.

BUTTRESSES

The huge weight of the cathedral tends to make the walls bulge outwards, whilst the lower parts of an arch cause a sideways force known thrust. **Buttresses** are thickened parts of the wall that help to prevent the building collapsing.

FLYING BUTTRESSES

Large buttresses get in the way of big windows, and can destroy the general elegance of the design. So some cathedrals have flying buttresses. These are buttresses that are constructed away from the main building, and which support the wall at its upper part.

THE CATHEDRAL

The traditional design of a cathedral is in the shape of a cross. The long limb is called the nave, and the cross-limb is the transept. Both nave and transept often had huge vaulted ceilings, and large windows to let in as much light as possible.

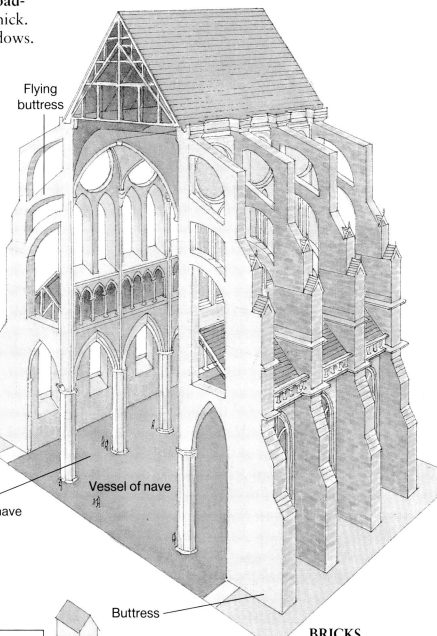

Flying buttress

Side aisle of nave

Vessel of nave

Buttress

Load

Flying buttress

Thrust

WATTLE AND DAUB

One old method of filling the spaces in-between the frame in a timber-framed building was wattle and daub. Thin pieces of wood were smeared with coatings of mud (wattle) or clay, and filled with straw (daub). These walls could take very little weight.

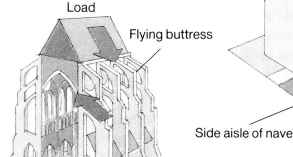

Daub

Wattle

Plaster lining

Foam in cavity

BRICKS AND CAVITIES

A brick wall can support enough weight for a building a few storeys high. There are usually two skins of brick, with an air gap between. The gap helps to keep out damp, and to insulate against temperature and noise. Filling materials such as foam help to improve the insulation.

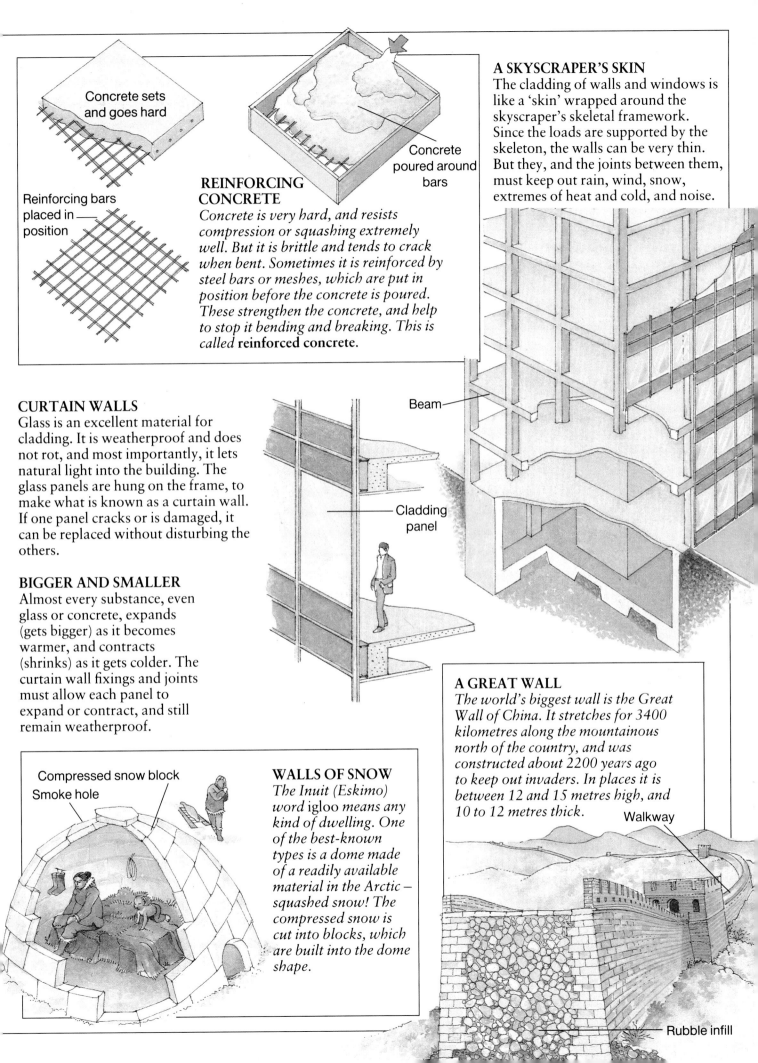

Concrete sets and goes hard

Reinforcing bars placed in position

Concrete poured around bars

REINFORCING CONCRETE

Concrete is very hard, and resists compression or squashing extremely well. But it is brittle and tends to crack when bent. Sometimes it is reinforced by steel bars or meshes, which are put in position before the concrete is poured. These strengthen the concrete, and help to stop it bending and breaking. This is called reinforced concrete.

A SKYSCRAPER'S SKIN

The cladding of walls and windows is like a 'skin' wrapped around the skyscraper's skeletal framework. Since the loads are supported by the skeleton, the walls can be very thin. But they, and the joints between them, must keep out rain, wind, snow, extremes of heat and cold, and noise.

Beam

CURTAIN WALLS

Glass is an excellent material for cladding. It is weatherproof and does not rot, and most importantly, it lets natural light into the building. The glass panels are hung on the frame, to make what is known as a curtain wall. If one panel cracks or is damaged, it can be replaced without disturbing the others.

Cladding panel

BIGGER AND SMALLER

Almost every substance, even glass or concrete, expands (gets bigger) as it becomes warmer, and contracts (shrinks) as it gets colder. The curtain wall fixings and joints must allow each panel to expand or contract, and still remain weatherproof.

A GREAT WALL

The world's biggest wall is the Great Wall of China. It stretches for 3400 kilometres along the mountainous north of the country, and was constructed about 2200 years ago to keep out invaders. In places it is between 12 and 15 metres high, and 10 to 12 metres thick.

Walkway

Compressed snow block
Smoke hole

WALLS OF SNOW

The Inuit (Eskimo) word igloo means any kind of dwelling. One of the best-known types is a dome made of a readily available material in the Arctic – squashed snow! The compressed snow is cut into blocks, which are built into the dome shape.

Rubble infill

Doors and windows

The electric light bulb was invented in about 1880, just over 100 years ago. For centuries before this, people relied on natural light from the Sun, and on the dim, flickering light from oily rags or oil lamps. So windows to let in natural light were vital. Even in a modern skyscraper, artificial lighting is not as pleasant as natural light. Windows also allow the people inside to look outside.

THE DOOR

In hot countries, doors are not needed to keep heat in a building. But a door does more than this. It keeps out rain, animals, flies and other pests, and unwanted visitors. It is also a symbol of ownership, showing that you are a guest on the owner's property.

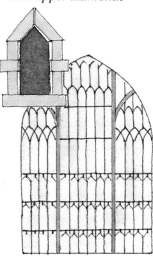

Two-panel sash windows slide up and down

Gothic arched window with upper diamonds

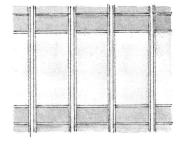

Panel window on curtain wall

Multi-panel casement window opens on hinges

Rectangular door with columns and horizontal lintel beam above

Gothic arched gateway and doorway

All-glass doors for good visibility and natural light

Byzantine door flanked by columns with stone arch above

PARTS OF A DOOR

A standard door is made of wood, as it was more than 1000 years ago. The parts should fit together exactly and stay firmly fixed. Otherwise the door sags and drags on the floor. It then becomes difficult to open and close.

Domestic door for typical house

Lift door

Revolving door

Sand

Lime

Sodium carbonate

Scrap glass

Furnace

GLASS
Glass is not a true solid. Technically it is known as a supercooled liquid. The main ingredients are sand (silica), limestone or lime (calcium carbonate), and sodium carbonate. These are heated in a furnace. The molten, runny glass is allowed to run into a shaped container, where it cools and hardens.

SASH WINDOW
A sash window slides up and down in grooves in its frame or box. It is steadied and held in place by sash cords that run around pulleys and connect to counterweights. The well-adjusted sash window stays as far up or down as you wish.

SECURITY
Sash windows are relatively secure against someone trying to force a way in, because the two parts can be locked against each other. A casement window that opens on hinges may be easier to force open, unless it has extra catches on the top and bottom.

COLOURED GLASS
Glass can be coloured by adding small amounts of coloured pigments when it is made. Copper pigments turn it blue, and selenium pigments make it red. Beautiful pictures and patterns can be made by fixing many small, shaped coloured panels into a stained glass-window. Many such windows are found in churches and cathedrals.

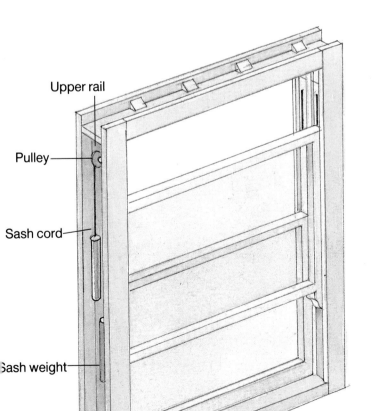

Upper rail

Pulley

Sash cord

Sash weight

Lower rail

Stairs and lifts

Without its lifts (elevators), a skyscraper would not be a practical building. People would spend far too much time and energy walking up and down stairs. The world's tallest building, the Sears Building in Chicago, has 102 lifts for people – some of them with double-decker cars – as well as other lifts for goods, services, security and emergencies.

THE ELEVATOR CAR

The elevator car has sliding doors that cannot open while the car is in motion. A bundle of flexible cables carries the electricity supply for the lights and doors, and the communications wires for the call buttons. The car has wheels that run in guide rails, or along steel cables. These wheels pass around pulleys, to stop the car swaying as it moves up and down.

CABLE LIFT

Most tall buildings have cable-operated lifts. A powerful electric motor winds the lifting cable on to a drum. This is not so difficult as it seems, since the main weight of the car is balanced by a counterweight. The lifting gear is usually in a small room on the top storey, or in a hut on the building's roof.

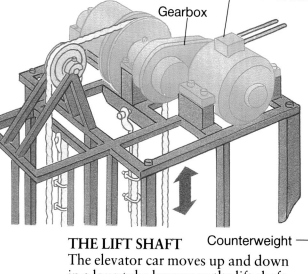

Electric winch motor

Gearbox

Counterweight cable

THE LIFT SHAFT

The elevator car moves up and down in a long tube known as the lift shaft. A small computer controls its movements, sending the car by the most economic route to the floors where the call buttons are pressed. **Hydraulic** safety buffers at the base of the shaft prevent the car from hitting the bottom.

Counterweight

Lobby sliding doors

Hydraulic piston

Floor buffers

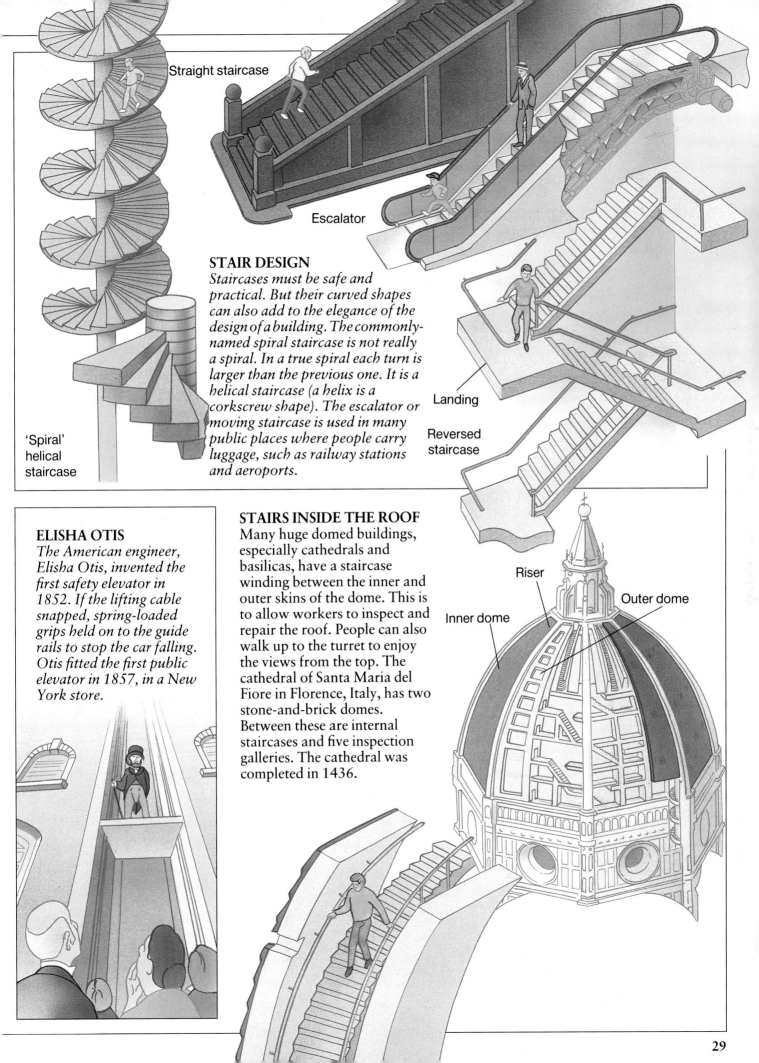

Straight staircase

Escalator

'Spiral' helical staircase

STAIR DESIGN

Staircases must be safe and practical. But their curved shapes can also add to the elegance of the design of a building. The commonly-named spiral staircase is not really a spiral. In a true spiral each turn is larger than the previous one. It is a helical staircase (a helix is a corkscrew shape). The escalator or moving staircase is used in many public places where people carry luggage, such as railway stations and aeroports.

Landing

Reversed staircase

ELISHA OTIS

The American engineer, Elisha Otis, invented the first safety elevator in 1852. If the lifting cable snapped, spring-loaded grips held on to the guide rails to stop the car falling. Otis fitted the first public elevator in 1857, in a New York store.

STAIRS INSIDE THE ROOF

Many huge domed buildings, especially cathedrals and basilicas, have a staircase winding between the inner and outer skins of the dome. This is to allow workers to inspect and repair the roof. People can also walk up to the turret to enjoy the views from the top. The cathedral of Santa Maria del Fiore in Florence, Italy, has two stone-and-brick domes. Between these are internal staircases and five inspection galleries. The cathedral was completed in 1436.

Riser

Outer dome

Inner dome

Roofs and roofing

Unless a building is covered by a watertight and weatherproof roof, then damp and rain will soon get inside, and gradually destroy the building. So the design and construction of a roof are vitally important. Roof checks and repairs are often put at the top of the maintenance list for a building. Modern materials, such as lightweight steel, glass, carbon fibres and special plastics, allow huge areas of roof to be covered.

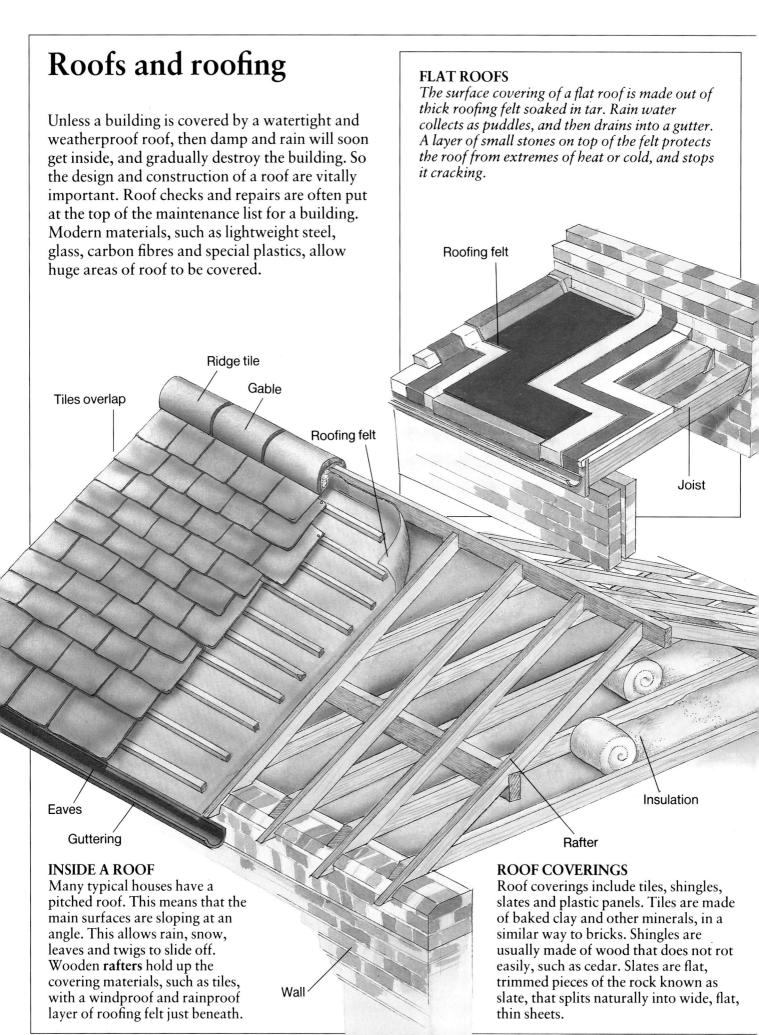

FLAT ROOFS
The surface covering of a flat roof is made out of thick roofing felt soaked in tar. Rain water collects as puddles, and then drains into a gutter. A layer of small stones on top of the felt protects the roof from extremes of heat or cold, and stops it cracking.

Roofing felt

Joist

Ridge tile

Gable

Tiles overlap

Roofing felt

Eaves

Guttering

Insulation

Rafter

Wall

INSIDE A ROOF
Many typical houses have a pitched roof. This means that the main surfaces are sloping at an angle. This allows rain, snow, leaves and twigs to slide off. Wooden **rafters** hold up the covering materials, such as tiles, with a windproof and rainproof layer of roofing felt just beneath.

ROOF COVERINGS
Roof coverings include tiles, shingles, slates and plastic panels. Tiles are made of baked clay and other minerals, in a similar way to bricks. Shingles are usually made of wood that does not rot easily, such as cedar. Slates are flat, trimmed pieces of the rock known as slate, that splits naturally into wide, flat, thin sheets.

ROOF DESIGNS

Various geometric shapes are used to span large areas of roof. A series of barrel vaults usually needs columns to support each vault. The name **hypar** *is a shortened version of the term hyperbolic paraboloid.*

Hypar or 'butterfly' roof

Barrel vault roof

BEAMS IN ROOFS

A triangle made from wooden beams or metal girders is much harder to bend out of shape than shapes such as squares or rectangles. So, the beams of a large pitched roof are designed in an interlinking pattern of small and large triangles to support the weight of the roof covering.

Tie beam

Arch braced roof-truss

Hammer beam roof-truss

THE SUPERDOME

Modern sports complexes are often spanned by gigantic domes, built of steel girders covered with roof cladding, or concrete panels. The curved surfaces allow the rain to trickle off. The biggest of these domes is the Louisiana Superdome, which measures 207 metres across.

HUNG ON WIRES

The modern suspended roof is light and weatherproof. But the support towers and cables must be checked regularly, to make sure they are not broken or corroded. In some cases the flexible roof material, such as reinforced plastic or fabric, has a limited life.

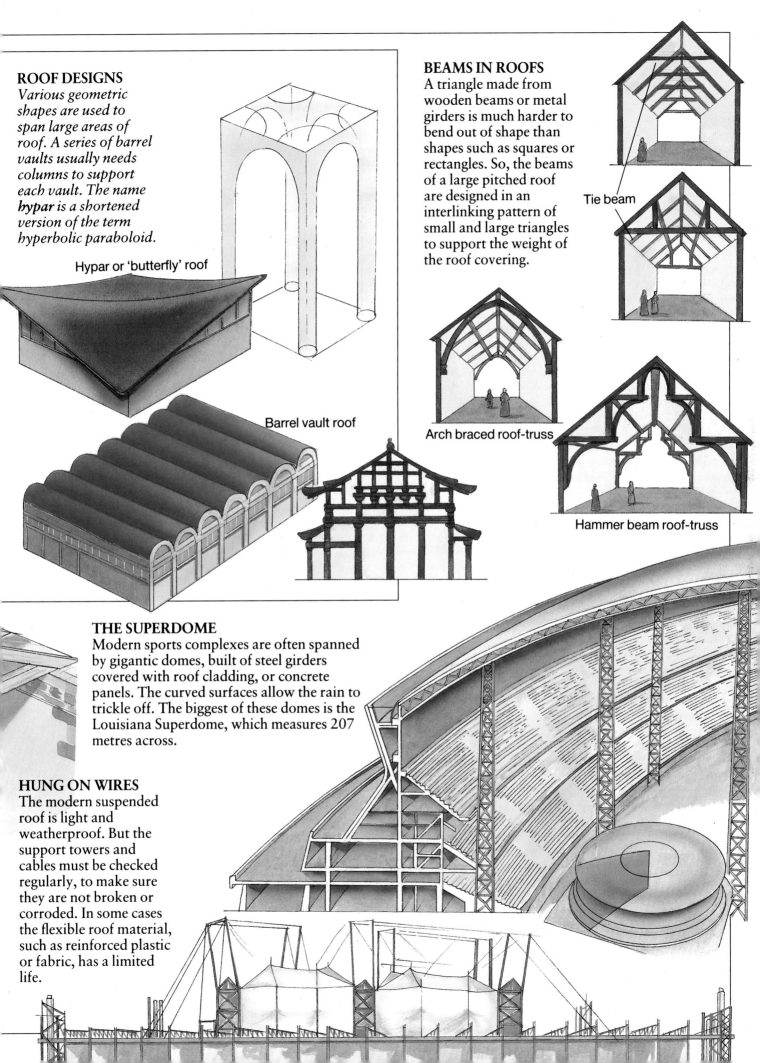

Water and plumbing

Water is not only used for drinking. A building needs a network of water and drainage pipes for sinks, basins, baths, showers, washrooms and lavatories, and for washing machines, dishwashers and other machines that require water. Some circuits carry cold water, others provide hot water. In a larger building water is needed to supply drinking fountains, **humidifiers** in the air-conditioning system, and **sprinkler systems** in case of fire.

THE COLD TANK

The cold tank is topped up continuously from the mains supply, through a ball valve. The metal or plastic ball floats on the water's surface. When the tank is full, the ball valve shuts down the water flowing in. If it doesn't work, an overflow pipe carries the extra water to the outside of the building.

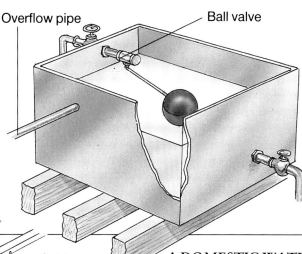

Overflow pipe

Ball valve

A DOMESTIC WATER SYSTEM

Cold water comes into a house along the high-pressure mains supply pipe. This empties into a cold-water tank in the roof space. The tank provides three low-pressure supplies: to the cold water taps, to the hot-water tank for the hot taps, and to the central heating system if this uses water-filled radiators.

WASTE WATER

In most areas, regulations state that water from sinks, basins, baths and showers must drain into one system, the waste pipes, while water from the lavatories goes into another system, the soil pipes. These two systems may join together outside the house, usually at the inspection chamber leading to the main sewage system.

Under most streets lies a network of water supply and sewage pipes, with branches to each house. A mains stopcock shuts off the entire water supply, in case of serious leaks.

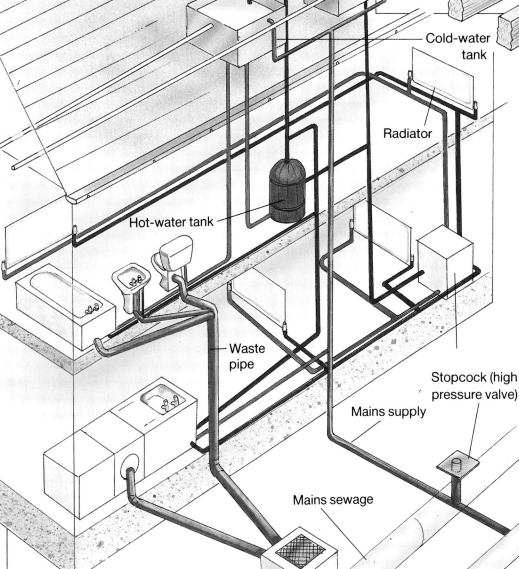

Central heating header tank

Cold-water tank

Radiator

Hot-water tank

Waste pipe

Stopcock (high pressure valve)

Mains supply

Mains sewage

A SPECIAL TAP

A **stopcock** *is a special type of tap, designed to withstand the high pressure of the water coming from the mains supply.*

Spindle

Rubber washer

Outlet

Overflow pipe

Ball valve

To pan

THE LAVATORY CISTERN

When the handle is pushed down, water is pulled by the sucking 'siphon' action around a U-shaped tube and down to the lavatory pan, washing it clean.

Lead

Damp sand

ROMAN PLUMBING

The Ancient Romans were experts at supplying clean water and taking away dirty water. Most Roman pipes were made of lead, which they called plumbum – *the origin of our word 'plumbing'. Roman pipes were made by wrapping lead around a piece of wood. A triangular piece of wood was used to make a groove in some damp sand. The pipe was put into the damp sand and liquid lead run along the groove to close up the open seam. This gave Roman lead pipes a ridge along the top.*

WATER IN A SKYSCRAPER

Normal pressure from the mains water supply is only strong enough to push water to a height of a few storeys. So in a tall building, electric pumps force the water higher, into storage tanks at various levels.

Roof level storage cistern

Intermediate level storage cistern

Cold water supply

Electric pumps

EARLY DRAINAGE

Mohenjo-daro is one of the cities built by the people of the Indus Valley, in present-day Pakistan, in about 2500 BC. The city had an efficient drainage system with drains underneath the streets to take waste water away. The Great Bath (*below*) had a drain nearly two metres deep, with a removable cover for inspection.

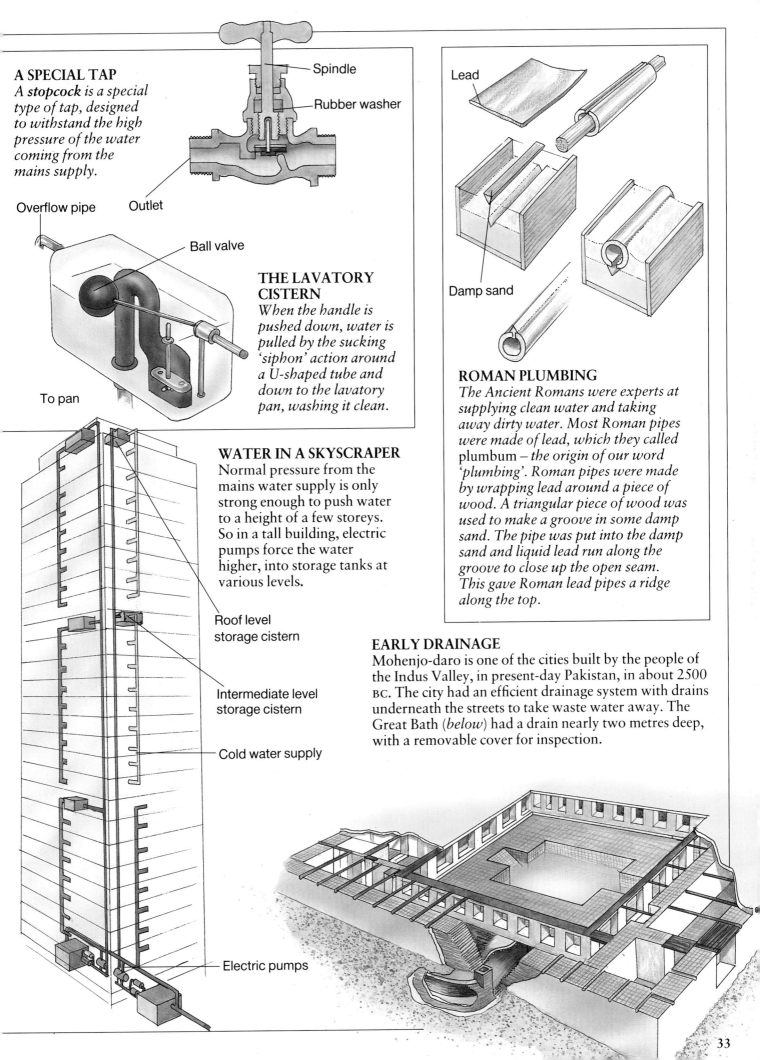

Electricity and services

In much of the world, modern life depends on electricity. From televisions to washing machines, lights to fans, electrical power drives many machines. However, mains electricity is also dangerous. It is invisible, and it can kill. So the electricity system in a building is subject to many rules and regulations. Gas supplies for heating and cooking (and occasionally lighting) are also controlled by safety regulations.

In most modern buildings, services such as electricity, gas, water, drainage and telecommunications are arranged into groups of pipes and cables. These pipes and cables lie in concealed ducts. This means that they are safely out of the way, yet engineers can get to them for repairs.

The architects of the Georges Pompidou Centre in Paris, France, decided to make a feature of the services in their building. All the service pipes are arranged along one wall on the outside of the building. Each one is brightly coloured according to its function.

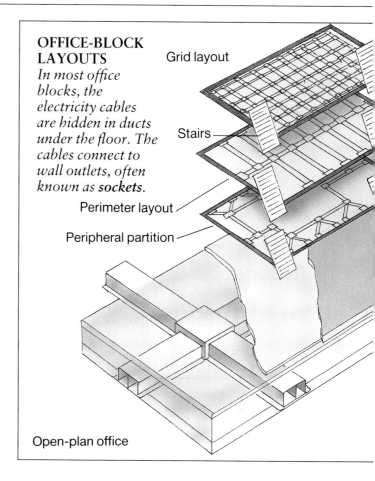

OFFICE-BLOCK LAYOUTS
In most office blocks, the electricity cables are hidden in ducts under the floor. The cables connect to wall outlets, often known as sockets.

Grid layout

Stairs

Perimeter layout

Peripheral partition

Open-plan office

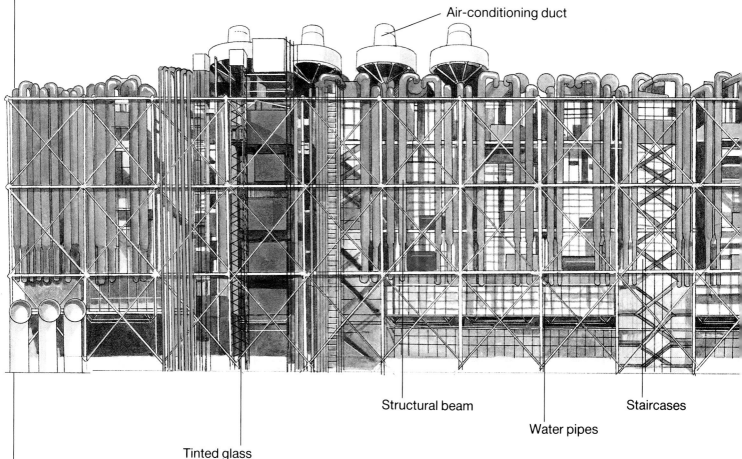

Air-conditioning duct

Structural beam

Water pipes

Staircases

Tinted glass

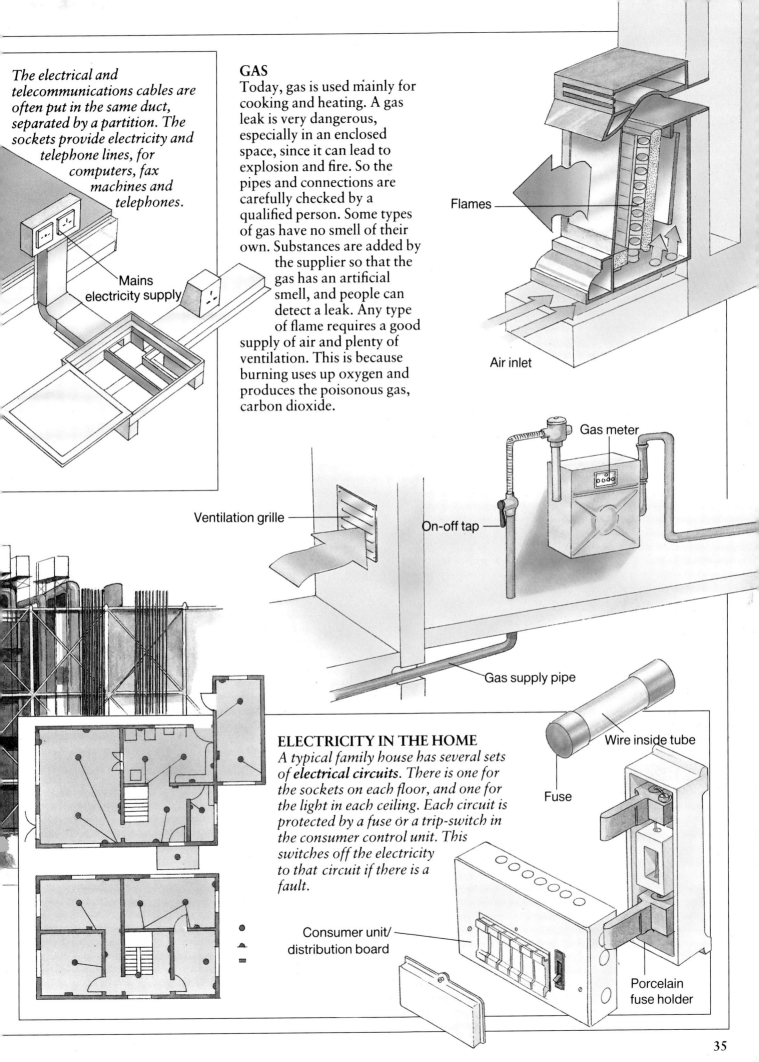

The electrical and telecommunications cables are often put in the same duct, separated by a partition. The sockets provide electricity and telephone lines, for computers, fax machines and telephones.

Mains electricity supply

GAS
Today, gas is used mainly for cooking and heating. A gas leak is very dangerous, especially in an enclosed space, since it can lead to explosion and fire. So the pipes and connections are carefully checked by a qualified person. Some types of gas have no smell of their own. Substances are added by the supplier so that the gas has an artificial smell, and people can detect a leak. Any type of flame requires a good supply of air and plenty of ventilation. This is because burning uses up oxygen and produces the poisonous gas, carbon dioxide.

Flames

Air inlet

Gas meter

Ventilation grille

On-off tap

Gas supply pipe

ELECTRICITY IN THE HOME
*A typical family house has several sets of **electrical circuits**. There is one for the sockets on each floor, and one for the light in each ceiling. Each circuit is protected by a fuse or a trip-switch in the consumer control unit. This switches off the electricity to that circuit if there is a fault.*

Wire inside tube

Fuse

Consumer unit/ distribution board

Porcelain fuse holder

Heating and air-conditioning

People like to have comfortable conditions in which to live their lives, whether they are at work or play, active or relaxed, awake or asleep. Otherwise they may begin to feel uncomfortably hot or cold, drowsy, or even sick or ill. So a building needs to have a fresh air supply, and to be kept at a reasonable temperature. Many buildings have a central heating system to heat the rooms during the winter.

ENERGY AND POLLUTION

Machines for heating and air-conditioning use up energy. Even electric heating, from the electricity supply, relies on energy being used up at the local power station. These machines may also pour polluting gases into the air. To save energy and to reduce pollution, buildings in cool climates have plenty of insulation to keep in the warmth.

AIR ON THE MOVE

In a building with spaces inside, such as a cinema or theatre, the air is kept on the move so that it carries away stale air and moisture vapour, smells and smoke. But the air should not move too fast, or the people inside will feel uncomfortable in the breeze!

An air-conditioning system controls the air that is going into a building. The system keeps the air smell-free, not too warm or cool, and not too dry or humid. The conditioned air flows gently along pipes and through inlet ducts into the main space. Fans pull the stale air through grilles and along pipes. Some of the air is recycled.

Air-conditioning machinery

Air flow

Floor extract grille

Extract duct

Stage

Chiller

Filter

Preheater

Dampers slow air flow

AIR-CONDITIONING SYSTEM

Thermostats in the building detect if the air is too cool or warm, or if it is too moist or dry. If the air is too cool it is warmed by the heater. If it is too hot it is cooled by the chiller. A spray of fine water moistens air that is too dry. In cold weather some of the warm air from inside the building is recycled, to save on heating.

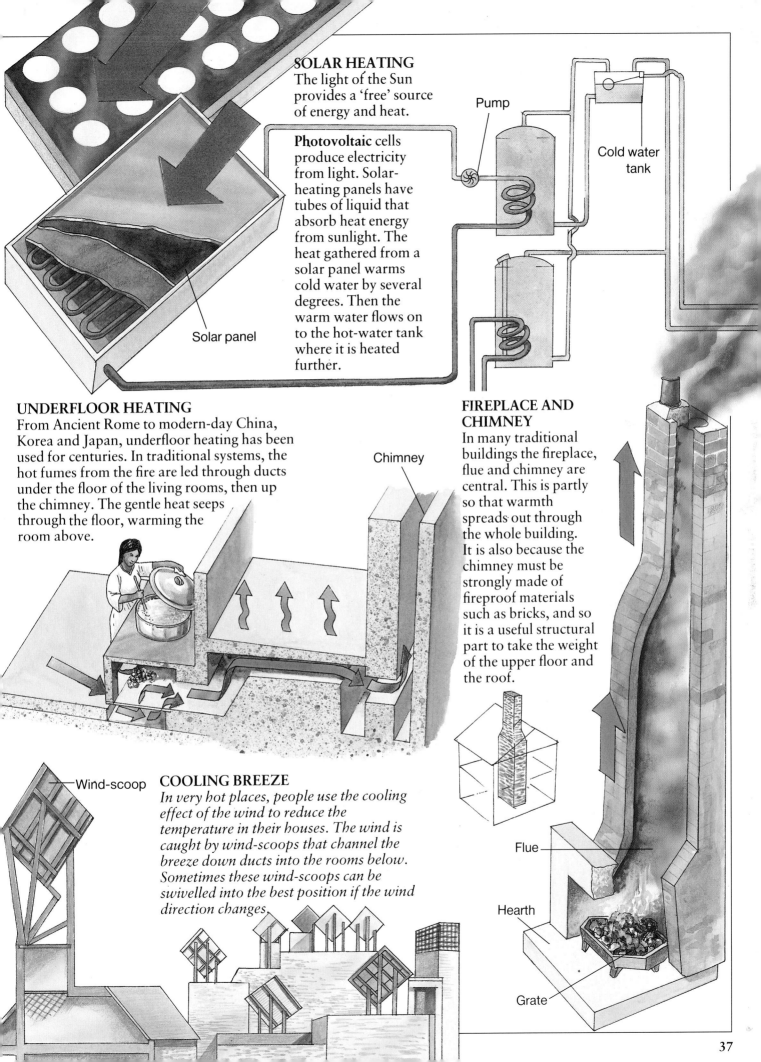

SOLAR HEATING
The light of the Sun provides a 'free' source of energy and heat.

Photovoltaic cells produce electricity from light. Solar-heating panels have tubes of liquid that absorb heat energy from sunlight. The heat gathered from a solar panel warms cold water by several degrees. Then the warm water flows on to the hot-water tank where it is heated further.

Pump

Cold water tank

Solar panel

UNDERFLOOR HEATING
From Ancient Rome to modern-day China, Korea and Japan, underfloor heating has been used for centuries. In traditional systems, the hot fumes from the fire are led through ducts under the floor of the living rooms, then up the chimney. The gentle heat seeps through the floor, warming the room above.

Chimney

FIREPLACE AND CHIMNEY
In many traditional buildings the fireplace, flue and chimney are central. This is partly so that warmth spreads out through the whole building. It is also because the chimney must be strongly made of fireproof materials such as bricks, and so it is a useful structural part to take the weight of the upper floor and the roof.

Flue

Hearth

Grate

Wind-scoop

COOLING BREEZE
In very hot places, people use the cooling effect of the wind to reduce the temperature in their houses. The wind is caught by wind-scoops that channel the breeze down ducts into the rooms below. Sometimes these wind-scoops can be swivelled into the best position if the wind direction changes.

Tunnels

Tunnels are useful for travel. They are far away from wind and rain. The people and vehicles passing through them can be controlled. There are few, if any, crossing points to delay the journey. But tunnels are expensive to excavate and maintain. Besides being used for travel, tunnels are made for many different functions – from water storage, to sewage disposal, to the latest scientific research.

Underground or subway trains run in tunnels beneath the city streets, avoiding delays in traffic jams and the problems of bad weather. This is why they are sometimes called rapid-transit systems. The New York Subway has 373 kilometres of track and 469 stations. The London Underground has more than 270 stations and 410 kilometres of track, but only some 170 kilometres are in tunnels. Safety is very important at a busy subway interchange. Thousands of passengers pass through the station every day. Staff check the signals, lighting and ventilation systems.

UNDERGROUND VENTILATION

In an underground system, the air soon goes stale. To overcome this problem there are wide shafts that connect the tunnels to the surface at regular intervals. They are positioned so that the moving trains pull fresh air down into the tunnels and stations, and push up stale air. The shafts also reduce the 'gale' felt by waiting passengers as a train approaches the station. Huge electric fans help to circulate the air.

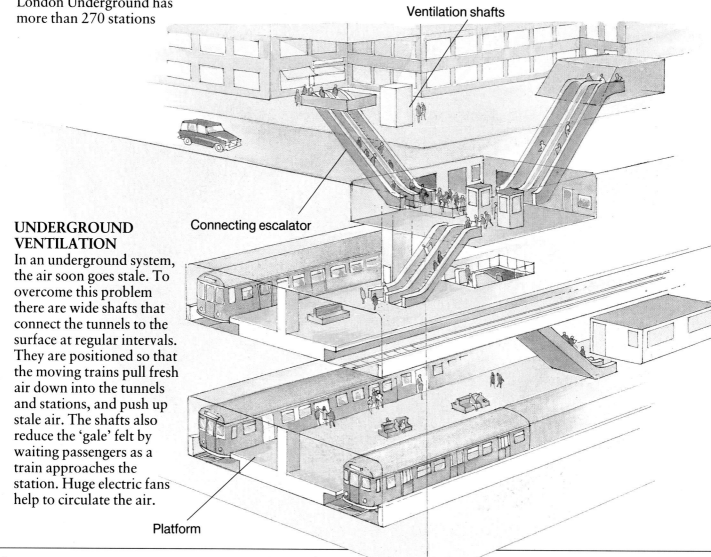

Ventilation shafts

Connecting escalator

Platform

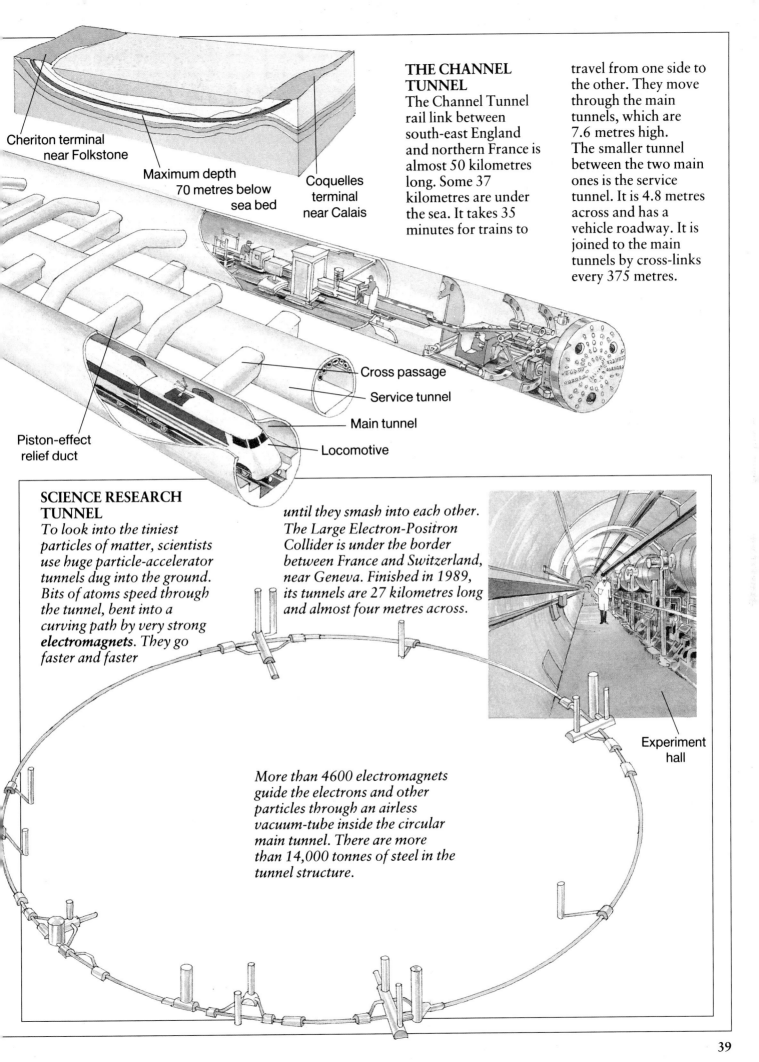

Cheriton terminal near Folkstone

Maximum depth 70 metres below sea bed

Coquelles terminal near Calais

Piston-effect relief duct

Cross passage

Service tunnel

Main tunnel

Locomotive

THE CHANNEL TUNNEL

The Channel Tunnel rail link between south-east England and northern France is almost 50 kilometres long. Some 37 kilometres are under the sea. It takes 35 minutes for trains to travel from one side to the other. They move through the main tunnels, which are 7.6 metres high. The smaller tunnel between the two main ones is the service tunnel. It is 4.8 metres across and has a vehicle roadway. It is joined to the main tunnels by cross-links every 375 metres.

SCIENCE RESEARCH TUNNEL

To look into the tiniest particles of matter, scientists use huge particle-accelerator tunnels dug into the ground. Bits of atoms speed through the tunnel, bent into a curving path by very strong electromagnets. They go faster and faster until they smash into each other. The Large Electron-Positron Collider is under the border between France and Switzerland, near Geneva. Finished in 1989, its tunnels are 27 kilometres long and almost four metres across.

Experiment hall

More than 4600 electromagnets guide the electrons and other particles through an airless vacuum-tube inside the circular main tunnel. There are more than 14,000 tonnes of steel in the tunnel structure.

Span that gap

Steep valleys and stretches of water have been barriers to human progress ever since ancient times. Early bridges were made out of materials such as wood and rope which tended to decay and weaken. Stone was used to construct bridges, but it was heavy to transport and build with. During the Industrial Revolution bridges were constructed from iron. Steel and reinforced concrete allow modern bridges to be much longer, yet lighter than the older designs.

SUSPENSION BRIDGES

At the entrance from the Pacific Ocean to San Francisco Bay, California, USA, stands the magnificent Golden Gate Bridge. Its six-lane roadway is hung from two main support cables, each 93 centimetres thick. These are strung from massive towers 227 metres high. The bridge was completed in 1937.

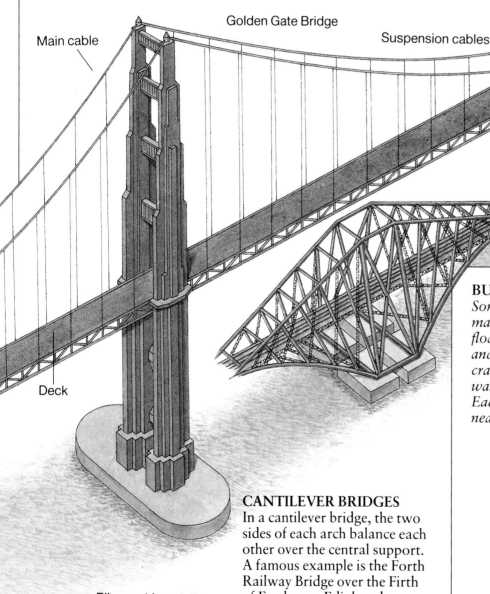

Main cable

Golden Gate Bridge

Suspension cables

Forth Railway Bridge

Deck

Piles and foundations

BUILT IN PLACE

Some cantilever bridges are constructed by making each arched span separately, then floating them into position on huge barges and lifting them into place with giant cranes. However, the Forth Railway Bridge was constructed piece by piece, in position. Each span became longer as it arched daily nearer its neighbour.

CANTILEVER BRIDGES

In a cantilever bridge, the two sides of each arch balance each other over the central support. A famous example is the Forth Railway Bridge over the Firth of Forth near Edinburgh, Scotland. It was one of the first large cantilever bridges to be constructed, in 1890. Made of steel, it is able to withstand strong winds.

ROPE BRIDGES

People have made fragile walkways of creepers, vines or twisted rope since prehistoric times, to cross gorges and ravines. The U-shaped walkway has wooden slats or a woven-net footpath, and rope handrails. This simple design was developed into a flat walkway of boards and rope railings, supported by a wood-beam trestle at each end. All of these natural materials had to be regularly maintained and replaced.

Guy ropes

Rope handrail

LIFTING BRIDGES

A vertical-lift bridge hoists the railway track or road out of the way, to allow ships through. The deck slots into channels in the support towers. The longest vertical-lift bridge is the Arthur Kill Railway Bridge between Staten Island and New Jersey, USA. It has a span of 170 metres, and was opened in 1959.

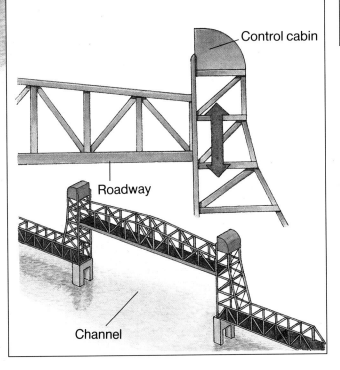

Control cabin

Roadway

Channel

BRIDGE BUSINESS

Bridges in big towns and cities channelled many people on to the same route. So they were ideal places for shops and other businesses. In Florence, Italy, the Ponte Vecchio still spans the River Arno, more than 600 years after it was first constructed. The shops on the bridge sell leather goods and glasswear to tourists.

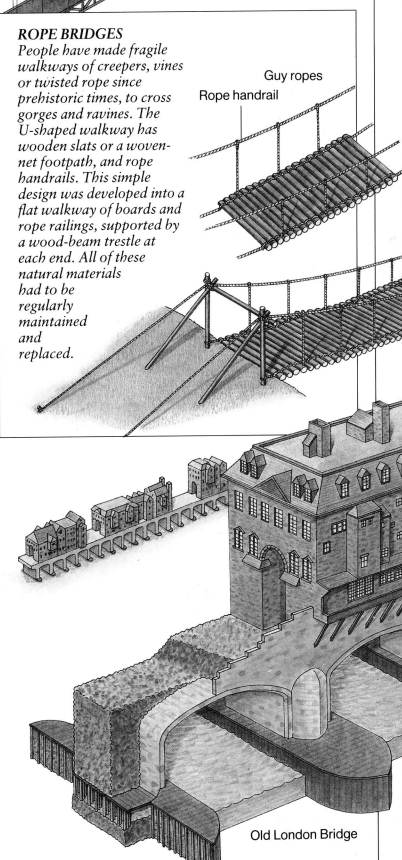

Old London Bridge

Ponte Vecchio

Great towns and cities often grew up by a major river. In medieval times, before iron and steel, stone bridges with many arches were often built to link the riverbanks.

Special buildings

There are great buildings all around the world. Some have particular or special uses. Others are constructed from unusual materials. Some are the first of a new style, or the last of an old one. Many are simply very beautiful. Here we look at a selection of special buildings which are used for different functions.

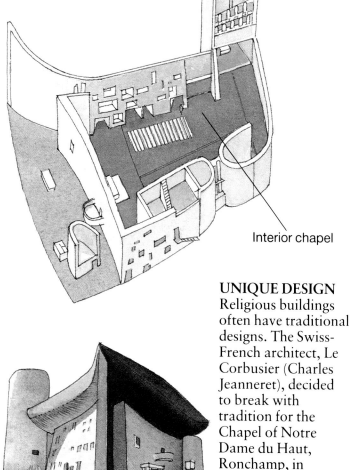

Interior chapel

ENCLOSING A SPACE

*The most efficient way to enclose the most space with the least surface is a sphere. In the 1950s, an American designer, Buckminster Fuller, developed this idea into the **geodesic** dome. The geodesic dome is made of many triangular panels which are light, yet strong. The **struts** between the panels can be made of almost any material, from bamboo to steel.*

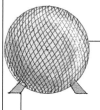

Outer skin

Tubular strut

Joint

UNIQUE DESIGN

Religious buildings often have traditional designs. The Swiss-French architect, Le Corbusier (Charles Jeanneret), decided to break with tradition for the Chapel of Notre Dame du Haut, Ronchamp, in southern France. The building has irregular windows and sweeping curves. It was completed in 1954.

Exterior chapel under roof overhang

PEOPLE AND PLANES

Airports are often mazes of corridors, walkways, lounges and gateways. However, the architects who designed the new Stansted Airport building, England, have tried to make the layout of the airport as simple as possible. The passenger terminal is all on one level. The services for the building are housed underneath the terminal. This means that there are no cables or ducts in the roof of the terminal. Instead, there are triangular rooflights that allow light in throughout the building. Passengers are taken to their planes by monorail trains.

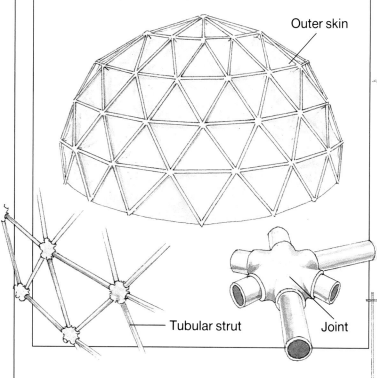

Departure lounge

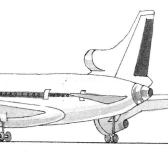

AN OIL RIG STRUCTURE

An oil rig is a structure rather than a building, even though crews come and go every few weeks. The biggest rigs are more than 200 metres high and weigh almost 1000 tonnes. Some are built on steel legs fixed to the sea bed. Others float, anchored by chains to weights.

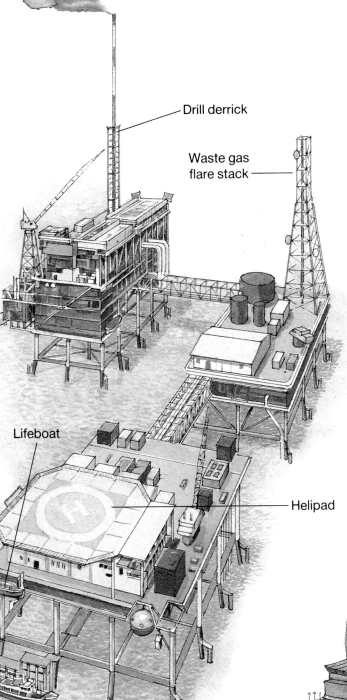

Drill derrick

Waste gas flare stack

Lifeboat

Helipad

Mooring jetty

Piles sunk into sea bed

FAMOUS BY DESIGN

One of the greatest sets of buildings from ancient times is the temple complex of Angkor Wat, Cambodia. It measured 1.5 kilometres long and 1.3 kilometres wide, with huge courtyards and 50 towers, some 50 metres high. The city fell into ruin from about 1225. It was rediscovered, hidden deep in the jungle, in the 1860s.

The Taj Mahal in Agra, India, is a tomb for the wife of the Mogul Emperor, Shah Jahan. It was completed in 1648.

SAILS IN THE HARBOUR

*The Sydney Opera House, Australia, is a striking design. It looks rather like the wind-filled sails of a ship, or a stack of sea shells. It is sited on a strip of land that juts out into Sydney Harbour. The original architect was Jorn Utzon from Denmark, and the building was finished in 1973. The main roof shape is made of pre-cast concrete sections, joined together in position, and covered by gleaming **ceramic** tiles.*

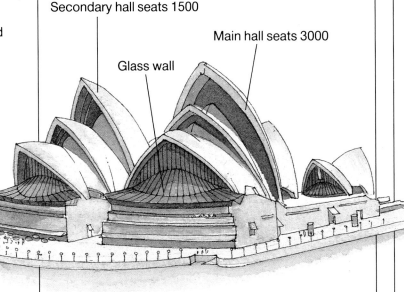

Secondary hall seats 1500

Main hall seats 3000

Glass wall

Glossary

air-conditioning The equipment that keeps the air in a building fresh, odour-free, and at a comfortable temperature, pressure and humidity for the people inside.

arch In its simplest form, an upside-down U shape that resists weight from above. There are many variations on the simple arch.

barrel vault A roof design that looks like a long, continuous arch.

buttress A strong pier or tower at the side of a building that resists the sideways forces of the roof and walls. It stops the building 'bulging' outwards and collapsing.

cement A mixture of limestone, clay and other substances that goes hard after it is mixed with water. It is a common building material in mortar and concrete.

ceramic A clay-based substance that can be made very hard and smooth, and which resists high temperatures and chemical corrosion.

cistern A tank, usually for water storage in the plumbing system of a building. It is often in the roof space or bathroom.

cladding Sheets of covering material, which can be made of glass, steel, plastic, wood or other substances. The steel framework of a large building is covered with cladding.

column A round, upright, supporting part, usually for the upper parts and roof of a building or other structure.

concrete A combination of cement, water, sand and small stones (aggregate). It can be poured into a shape and then sets very hard, and it is used in many buildings and structures.

crypt A room, usually underground, in a church or similar building. It is used for worship or as a burial place. (The name comes from a Greek word meaning 'hidden or secret'.)

dome A curved structure, the most common form being like half of a ball or sphere. Domes are generally used as roofs.

duct A long hole, like a pipe or tunnel, but usually square or rectangular. It can be used for air circulation, or as the routeway for electrical wires, water pipes and other services.

electrical circuit In general terms, the wires that carry electricity around a building or other structure.

electromagnet A magnet worked by electicity, that can be switched on and off.

footings The supporting parts of a building below ground level, usually tracing out the pattern of the walls.

foundations The whole set of supporting parts of a building below ground level.

geodesic To do with curved shapes and curved surfaces.

girder A strong, long supporting part, especially made of steel, iron or concrete.

humidifier A device that adjusts the amount of moisture (invisible water vapour) in the air, so that people do not feel it is too dry, or too moist.

hydraulic Worked by fluid (usually a special oil, or water) under pressure.

hypar Short for hyperbolic paraboloid, a curved surface shaped like a horse's saddle or a butterfly poised for take off.

joist A beam or similar long, strong part used to support a floor or roof.

load-bearing wall A wall that bears or supports the load – the weight of the parts above it, including the upper walls and floors, and the roof. (In many tall buildings the steel framework supports most of the weight.)

mezzanine An intermediate floor or storey, like a large balcony or landing, that goes only part of the way across a room or building.

mullion The main upright or vertical part (or parts) in a window.

photovoltaic An electronic device that turns light into electricity, as in a solar panel or light-powered calculator.

pier In buildings, a base or supporting part for a column or pillar, or the part of a wall between two large openings.

piles Long, strong parts, like underground pillars, that go deep into the earth to support the weight of a tall building.

rafter A long, strong part of a roof, usually like a sloping beam, that holds up the main roof covering.

reinforced concrete Concrete with steel rods, mesh, beams or girders in it, to give it extra strength (especially when stretched).

services The supplies of electricity, water, air, telephone and computer cables, and other requirements of a building. In a large building they are usually grouped together.

socket The thing you push a plug into. A mains electrical wall socket is for a standard electrical plug, and is also called a wall outlet.

sprinkler system A network of water pipes and sprayers, that switches on in an emergency to dampen and extinguish any fire.

stopcock A water tap in the main supply pipe, that shuts off the water to all (or a large part) of the plumbing system.

strut A short supporting part, that usually holds one piece away from another.

thermostat A sensor that detects temperature and turns the heating or cooling system on or off, to maintain a constant temperature.

vault A long arch. The simplest type is the barrel vault, which is straight and has no connections to other vaults.

Index